Ravenscourt
B·O·O·K·S

Entrepreneurs

By

C. L. Collins

W9-BDN-113

SRA

Columbus, OH

SRAonline.com

 SRA

Send all inquiries to this address:
SRA/McGraw-Hill
4400 Easton Commons
Columbus, OH 43219

Printed in the United States of America.

ISBN: 978-0-07-612170-0
MHID: 0-07-612170-4

      4 5 6 7 8 9 MAL 13 12 11 10 09

The **McGraw·Hill** Companies

Contents

—Chapter 1—

What Is an Entrepreneur?

Entrepreneur is a word we often hear. In the United States, entrepreneurs are the heart of the economy. But what does it mean? *Entrepreneur* comes from a French word, *entreprendre,* which means "to undertake." *Entrepreneurs* are people willing to undertake a new business. They are willing to find a new solution to a problem and then bring that solution into the market. And they are willing to take great risks to do it. Entrepreneurs like to work for themselves. They are willing to work hard too. They take the blame for failures and the praise for successes.

Success means different things to different entrepreneurs. Some want to be the biggest in their field. Some choose a small area and wish to do well in just that area. Some sell millions of things. Some sell only one thing. But they all want to turn their ideas into reality.

As you read* about these entrepreneurs, think about the choices they made and the risks they faced. Their paths to success were never easy. Many made mistakes, but they never stopped working toward their goals.

Chapter 2

"Mrs. Knox Says"

At the turn of the 20th century, many people used new technology to prepare food. There were new ways to do work in factories. For example, Clarence Birdseye experimented with freezing foods. C. W. Post made cereals. J. T. Dorrance did well selling Campbell's condensed soups in cans. And they all used the method Henry Ford used to make cars—an assembly line.

Charles Knox was a glove salesman. He often watched his wife Rose make gelatin at home. She would boil beef bones for many hours to remove the marrow from the bones. This was then used to make the gelatin. Because gelatin was so time-consuming to make, few people ate it.

Mr. Knox and his wife were married in 1883. They often decided together what they should do. But Mrs. Knox's main job was being a housewife. She liked to cook. She spent most of her time raising their children. And she managed all the money for the household.

In 1890 the two decided to build a gelatin business. They thought they could make a granulated gelatin that would be easy for people to use at home. They used 5,000 dollars of their savings to buy a factory for their new business—Knox Gelatine.

The Knoxes spent almost all their money on the factory, so Mr. Knox had to keep his job as a traveling glove salesman. On the side, he would sell gelatin. His wife and two sons often went with him on sales trips. That way, they could learn the gelatin business.

But the Knoxes had a problem with their product. Because gelatin was hard to make, most people weren't used to eating it. At that time, gelatin was eaten mostly by people who were ill.

The Knoxes had to create *demand*. They had to explain to customers how and why they should use Knox Gelatine. So in 1896 Mrs. Knox wrote a little cookbook called *Dainty Dessert.* It was filled with gelatin recipes. Soon one million copies of the cookbook were being given away each year.

Mr. Knox tried to tell people about Knox Gelatine in flashy ways. He bought a racehorse and named it Gelatine King. He bought a blimp with the word *Gelatine* on it in big letters, and it flew around the country. Mr. Knox also bought different businesses, like a hardware store and a newspaper.

In 1908, after 18 years in the gelatin business, Mr. Knox died. Mrs. Knox had to decide what to do. Should she sell the business? Should she hire someone to manage it? Her two sons were too young to take over the family business. No one thought she would keep it. Women did not run big companies at that time.

But, at age 50, Mrs. Knox decided to keep the business and run it herself. She knew many people would not accept a woman in business. So she sent cards to her husband's former business partners. She told them she was taking over the company only until her first son was old enough to take over.

But at the factory, Mrs. Knox let people know from the first day that she was not afraid to make changes. She politely asked for the resignation of one manager who said he could never work for a woman.

Mrs. Knox changed the business in important ways. She sold off her husband's other businesses. Then she changed the way Knox Gelatine was advertised and sold. Mrs. Knox knew most gelatin buyers were women. So she advertised to them. She said gelatin was healthy and did not cost much. She put recipes on the gelatin boxes. She created advertisements that looked like a newspaper column called "Mrs. Knox Says."

To find new markets, Mrs. Knox created a research kitchen to experiment with gelatin. This led to gelatin being used in the photo and medical industries. For example, gelatin covering was used on pills to make them easier to swallow. This was an early type of "gel cap."

Mrs. Knox also did something far ahead of her time. In 1913 she set a five-day work week. She also gave workers a two-week vacation each year and time off when they were sick.

Rose Knox prepares for a party to celebrate her 80th birthday and her 30th year as head of Knox Gelatine

*The business kept growing. Soon she built a new factory. Then she built a second factory. From 1908 to 1915, the value of Knox Gelatine tripled. The hardest time was during the Great Depression. Many businesses closed and many people were put out of work. But Mrs. Knox never laid off a single employee. She even created a new line of flavored gelatin. The business even got bigger.

In 1947, on her 90th birthday, she stepped aside so her son could become president of the company. But she remained chairman of the board. When she died in 1950, Mrs. Knox was thought of as the most important female industrialist in the United States.

Robert García and his wife Margaret worked as sales managers at a big food company in California. It made lots of different things. In 1982 the Garcías decided to start a company of their own. They decided* they would distribute one thing: snack foods.

With 1,000 dollars in savings, the Garcías rented a small warehouse and found someone to make their products. Then the Garcías loaded up their van and drove around doing what they did best—selling. They wanted to work only three days a week. After a few months, the Garcías were working a lot more than three days a week. So they bought more vans and hired some employees.

The business was doing well and growing. Then a disaster struck. Their manufacturer told them it forgot to print the bags that said "R. W. García." The Garcías would have to wait six weeks for the bags to be printed and filled. For a food supplier, having to wait six weeks could easily destroy the business.

The Garcías discovered that by manufacturing the product themselves, they could have more control of their products. They could also control costs better.

So the Garcías borrowed 300,000 dollars from friends and family. In 1986 they opened their own manufacturing plant. But they suddenly learned an important lesson. Selling and making are two very different things.

In Philadelphia, Pennsylvania, Mr. García found the machines he wanted. He paid workers to take them apart and drive them to California. Then he raced home to rent a new space for the machines.

Soon the trucks with the machines arrived. But Mr. García had forgotten to get a forklift to take the machines off the trucks. Then the Garcías discovered something else. They didn't know what to do with the machines. They didn't know how to put them together. There were no manuals or instructions.

For six months, Mr. García learned how to solder, drill, weld, and thread pipes to make the machines work. When the day for the grand opening came, there was a big party.

Mr. García decided to make the first batch of tortilla chips himself. Unfortunately, they were terrible. The Garcías had to experiment for six more months before they made the tortilla chips they wanted to sell.

The Garcías made organic tortilla chips. They hoped more and more people would want to buy natural and organic foods. They also saw that organic foods were finding their way into big chain supermarkets. So they decided to focus on the organic section of the market to set them apart from other tortilla makers. The Garcías were the first to make the popular organic "blue" tortilla chips.

After a few years, their company's sales were over one million dollars a year. In 1997 they opened a second plant in Florida. That way they could sell on the East Coast and export to Europe too. Then they opened a third plant. Their hope that more and more people would buy organic tortilla chips paid off.

—Chapter 3—

The Beauty Business

For centuries, women worked at home. Only a very, very few had businesses. But there is one type of business in which women have always done well—making and selling beauty products. And there are many interesting women who went into the beauty business.

Two early competitors in the beauty business were Sarah Walker and Annie Turnbo Malone. In 1867 Walker was born in Louisiana. Her parents died when she was six. Walker got married when she was 14 years old and had a baby a few years later. Her husband was killed when she was 20, so she and her two-year-old daughter moved up the Mississippi River to St. Louis, Missouri. Walker was an African American woman who did not know how to read and write. Her choices were limited. She took a job washing clothes.

For years Walker pounded and rubbed clothes for hours every day. The hot water and detergents made her hair fall out. She started to experiment with different products, trying to find something that would help. Sometime after 1900 she created her special hair formula. She also developed a special hot comb. She said they were to help women grow their hair. But most African American women used them to straighten their hair.

In 1905, when she was 38, she moved to Denver, Colorado. There she married Charles J. Walker. He worked in the newspaper business. He helped her advertise her products and change her image. She took one of his suggestions and started to use the name "Madame C. J. Walker" on her products. Walker went door to door selling her hair treatment. Soon she trained others to sell her hair-care system. The saleswomen dressed in white shirts and long black skirts.

Madame C. J. (Sarah) Walker

In 1910 Walker moved her manufacturing plant to Indianapolis, Indiana. There she also built a research lab and a beauty school. In Indianapolis she was closer to most of her clients—African American women who lived in the South, North, and East. Walker became famous. When she died in 1919, she had become the first female African American millionaire.

Malone was next to the youngest of 11 children. Her parents were former enslaved people. After they died, she lived with her older siblings. When she was in high school she started to experiment in the school's chemistry lab. She wanted to make an ointment for women's hair that would soften it. She became ill, though, and could not finish school. But that didn't stop her. In 1900 she made her special ointment in the back of a building in Lovejoy, Illinois. The building was across the river from St. Louis.

In 1902 Malone moved to St. Louis just as plans for the World's Fair were being made. She knew thousands of people would soon pass through the city. So she worked to let people know about her hair product. She went door to door selling her ointment, the Wonderful Hair Grower. She hired assistants to help sell it. She held press conferences. Soon her products were being sold all over the Midwest. In 1903 Malone married. But she soon divorced her husband when he tried to interfere in her hair-care business.

Some people say Walker had worked for Malone and copied Malone's formula. In 1906 Malone copyrighted her hair products, which she named Poro. She advertised in African American newspapers. She traveled across the country giving demonstrations of her products. Soon there were many imitators selling their own hair straighteners and hot combs.

Malone expanded her business. In 1917 she built a big building in St. Louis. In it there was a beauty school with a dormitory, plus the factory and a store. The beauty school, named Poro College, interested women from all over the country. There, students learned to use Poro products. They also learned many other skills. Malone opened Poro Colleges all over the United States. In 1926 the company said there were 26,000 Poro College salespeople working in the United States and the Caribbean. In the 1920s, Malone was one of the richest African American women in the United States.

Malone had married Aaron Malone in 1914. In 1927 he sued for divorce. He wanted half of her business. After the bitter divorce, Malone's business began to decline. In 1930 she moved the business to Chicago, Illinois, where she bought an entire city block. Malone died in 1957.

Two more fierce competitors were Elizabeth Arden and Helena Rubinstein. They were both businesswomen.

Around 1878 Elizabeth Arden, whose real name was Florence Graham, was born to a farming family in Canada. Her mother died when she was very young. She dropped out of high school to help support the family. She worked as a nurse, as a dentist's assistant, and in many other jobs.

In 1908 Arden moved to New York City. She got a job as a cashier at a beauty salon. She was about 30 years old, but people said she looked like she was 20. Arden asked her employer to show her how to give facials. Soon she had her own clients who came for her "healing hands." In 1910 Arden opened her own salon on Fifth Avenue. She named it Elizabeth Arden. She also started calling herself by that name.

Arden had borrowed 6,000 dollars from her brother to open the salon. She also got a small loan from the bank. She never had to borrow money again.

Arden was going into the beauty business as the world was changing. For many years, "high-class" women did not wear makeup. As times changed, however, more and more women wanted to use makeup and beauty products.

Arden wanted her salon to appeal to wealthy women. She decorated it as beautifully as she could, and she painted the door red. In her salon, women could be pampered. They could have all kinds of special treatments like facials and massages. Soon she was selling her own brand of creams, lotions, and makeup. She advertised her products in newspapers and glossy magazines. Over 50 Elizabeth Arden salons opened across the United States and Europe. They all had the trademark red door.

Arden liked to be called "Mrs. Arden." She thought her clients would have more confidence in her if they thought she was married. Arden was well dressed and had a youthful beauty. She owned 100 percent of the company, and she stayed in control of the company to the end of her life. She worked until the day she died in 1966. She was nearly 90 years old.

Helena Rubinstein was born in 1870 in Poland. Her father wanted her to be a doctor. But she got sick whenever she worked in the lab. Then her father said she must marry an older widower. She said she wouldn't. She asked to move to Australia. She took with her the special pots of cream her mother's friend, a famous actress, used.

*In Australia, Rubinstein gave away the cream as gifts. She noticed that the harsh sun there damaged the skin of many women. She quickly saw a business opportunity. So Rubinstein borrowed money and opened a small shop. She started to experiment with different kinds of creams. She also traveled to Europe to consult with skin-care experts. Her business boomed.

In Europe she met an American newspaperman. He asked her to marry him. She told him he had to wait until she opened a salon in London, England. Only then did she marry. Soon she had two children. When her youngest child was two, she opened a salon in Paris, France. Rubinstein and her husband moved to the United States in 1914. Then she opened a salon in New York City.

Rubinstein's products became very popular when famous stars started to use them. She began opening salons across the United States.*

There were very few women who had such large and profitable businesses. But Rubinstein found it hard to expand her business while having a family. So in 1928 she decided to sell her business. She sold it for over seven million dollars. The stock market crashed the next year, and she bought the company back for one and a half million dollars. But her marriage soon ended.

Rubinstein expanded her empire. She became one of the world's richest women. She had turned the small pots of cream into gold. Rubinstein worked until she died in 1965. She was 94 years old.

Rosie Herman was a manicurist in Texas. When she had twin daughters, she stopped working to stay home with them. Her hands became red and raw, mostly from doing so much washing.

Herman tried to make something in her kitchen she could use on her hands. She needed something that wouldn't hurt her children while she was feeding them.

Herman's sister gave her a gift of an oil-and-salt scrub. Herman looked carefully at the list of ingredients. She felt she could make her own scrub that would be better than the oil-and-salt scrub.

Herman bought the ingredients she needed at the grocery store and made a batch of scrub. Then she gave jars of the scrub away as Christmas gifts. People began asking for more of it. So she started to sell it. It was called "Mommy's Magic." She went to craft fairs on weekends and sold jars of her scrub for 25 dollars.

But Herman didn't have enough money to buy supplies. She went to the bank to borrow money to expand the business, but she was turned down. She and her husband were already deeply in debt. They had spent tens of thousands of dollars on doctors' bills. So she borrowed money from her sister to buy supplies.

As the business grew, she moved production from her kitchen to her garage. Her husband quit his job to work for her. She gave the product a catchy new name—One Minute Manicure. Then a few local salons began to sell her scrub.

That was in 1999. By 2004 she had her own factory and had sold 20 million dollars worth of scrub.

—Chapter 4—

Good News Travels Fast

How do you get your information? For some entrepreneurs, finding new ways to collect and organize information was the center of their business.

Edward W. Scripps was born in 1854 in a small Illinois town. He read a lot as a boy. But he left school when he was 15 to work on his family's farm. When he was 19 he went to work for his older half-brother John. John had just opened a newspaper called the *Detroit Evening News*. Scripps worked there for five years and learned all about the newspaper business. First he helped distribute the newspaper. Then he wrote for it. Later he became an editor. But Scripps wanted to make his own business, away from his brother's shadow. He had his own ideas about how to run a newspaper.

Scripps started the *Cleveland Penny Press* in 1878. The paper cost one cent. It was instantly popular. Later Scripps said he learned there that if the newspaper was filled with many small items, it sold very well. But he wanted to do more than run a single newspaper. He wanted to own a chain of newspapers.

Scripps started a newspaper in St. Louis in 1880 and another one in Cincinnati, Ohio, a year later. Scripps then bought newspapers in San Francisco and Los Angeles, California. His idea was to keep costs low by using many of the same articles in different newspapers. Up to that time, newspapers were all locally owned. Each newspaper created its own material.

By the late 1890s, Scripps had started his own telegraph news service. He thought stories could be sent quickly by telegraph—"over the wires"—to newspapers around the country.

In this way, Scripps used new technology to send information. There were no telephones, radios, or televisions then. In 1902 Scripps started a "features" service. The service sold photos, cartoons, stories, and other information to newspapers. He was the first to do so. This was another way to keep costs low.

Scripps bought or opened a total of 29 newspapers. His newspapers had a strong point of view. He kept prices low to appeal to more readers. And his newspapers were very profitable. When he retired in 1922 he had forever changed the way newspapers were owned and operated. He died in 1926.

Like Scripps, John H. Johnson was also born in a small town. Johnson was born in Arkansas in 1918.

*As a young African American in the South, Johnson went to a segregated school. His father worked at a sawmill. He died in an accident there when Johnson was eight years old. There was no public high school for African Americans where Johnson lived. But he loved to learn so much he went to eighth grade a second time. Finally he and his mother moved to Chicago, where he went to high school. Johnson was a country boy in a big city. Other students often teased him. But he pushed himself harder. He became an honor student, editor of the school newspaper, and student council president.

Johnson did so well that he was invited to speak at the Urban League, an African American group. Johnson's speech impressed a man named Harry Pace. Pace was president of the Supreme Liberty Life Insurance Company. It was the biggest African American-owned business in* the United States. Pace offered Johnson a job and a college scholarship.

Johnson started as an office clerk. After two years he was Pace's personal assistant. One of his many jobs was to read newspapers and magazines to find articles that would be interesting to African Americans. He would then tell Pace what he had read. That way Pace could keep up with what was happening in the community. Johnson soon had an idea. Caucasian readers loved magazines like *Reader's Digest*. Why not put together a magazine like that for African American readers? There weren't any magazines for African American readers then. There were only a few stories about African Americans in magazines like *Life* and *Time*.

Johnson looked for investors to help him start the magazine. Everyone told him it was a bad idea. He couldn't find anyone, African American or Caucasian, to lend him any money. So he had to find another way to raise money.

Johnson wrote to all of Pace's insurance customers. He told them that for two dollars they could have a subscription to a new magazine, *Negro Digest*. From that letter he received 3,000 subscriptions. Johnson then found someone who would lend him the 500 dollars he needed for postage to mail the magazines.

Johnson had to get newsstands to carry the new magazine. He wanted them to think it was a very popular new magazine, so he asked his friends to buy all the copies of the magazine they could find. And he lent them money to do it. That was in November 1942. Six months later, 50,000 copies of *Negro Digest* were in circulation each month.

Next Johnson decided to publish a magazine about African American entertainment news. The most popular magazine in the United States at the time was *Life*. Johnson decided to make his new magazine look like *Life*.

In 1945 the first copies of *Ebony* were published. It was an instant success. Later, in 1951, the weekly newsmagazine *Jet* first appeared.

Johnson's biggest problem in the first years was always advertising. Magazines and newspapers make most of their money from advertising. But Johnson could not get large, Caucasian-owned businesses to advertise in a magazine for African Americans. They did not think it would be profitable.

To make up for lack of advertising, Johnson started a mail-order company named Beauty Star. Beauty Star sold beauty products like wigs. Johnson advertised the company in his magazines. Beauty Star finally became Fashion Fair Cosmetics, a line of makeup for African American women that is still very profitable.

Johnson wanted big companies like the television maker Zenith to advertise in *Ebony*. He did not have any luck at first.

Then Johnson found out the chairman of Zenith was interested in polar exploration. So Johnson found Matthew Henson, an African American who had traveled with Robert Peary to the North Pole. Johnson asked Henson for a copy of his autobiography and asked him to sign it. Johnson then sent the book as a gift to the chairman of Zenith. The chairman soon placed ads in Johnson's magazines. He also called other big advertisers, who did the same thing. By 1948 *Ebony* was profitable.

Johnson Publishing Company grew into a large and profitable publishing empire. It went into radio and television. It was one of the largest African American-owned businesses in the United States. Johnson died in 2005, 60 years after the first issue of *Ebony* appeared.

Cathy Hughes grew up in Omaha, Nebraska. Education was always important to her family. Her grandfather had picked out a college for her and had paid for her to go. But her life changed when she got pregnant at age 16. She got married. As a new mother, she lost her dream of going to college. After a few years, she divorced. Then she moved to Washington, D.C., to help her father open a business. It was 1971.

Hughes went to work at the Communications Department at Howard University. In two years she was the sales manager of the college radio station, WHUR. After a few more years she was running the station. She created a popular show called *The Quiet Storm* that played romantic songs at night. The style of the show was copied all over the country.

In 1978 Hughes remarried. The next year she and her husband wanted to buy an AM radio station, WOL. It was small, with only 1,000 watts. But their problem was money. They needed one and a half million dollars to buy the station. Hughes knew all about radio operations. Her husband knew what he wanted to do with the station. But they didn't know how to run a profitable business.

Hughes later said the first time a lender asked her what her business plan was, she said, "My plan is to become successful." The would-be investors laughed. "I was embarrassed and intimidated, but I was determined to learn,"[1] she said. She traveled to banks all over the country looking for a loan. She was told no 32 times. Finally she found a loan officer who would take a chance on her.

Hughes wanted to create a news and talk station for African American listeners. She had market research that showed African American listeners were an untapped market for advertisers. But finding advertisers was hard. After a few years her marriage ended, and she was left to manage the station on her own. She also had to repay the loan.

Hughes had to learn quickly. She found out she needed to learn how to be a good entrepreneur before anything else. One of the first things she learned was that banks only cared about a return on their investment.

The bank demanded that Hughes start playing music to cut costs. News and talk shows cost more than just playing music. So she made a deal. She kept talk shows on in the morning and played music for the rest of the day.

Without money to pay a DJ, Hughes went on the air herself. She stayed on the air for 14 years. But there were some very hard times. One day she looked out the window and saw her car being repossessed. For a while she couldn't pay rent and had to sleep at the radio station.

Hughes's son, Alfred, went to work at the station as a salesman in 1985. By 1986 the station had turned its first profit. In 1987 Hughes bought her second station. Her strategy was to buy urban stations that weren't performing well. Then she would make them profitable by giving them new formats for African American listeners. Her son got an MBA, and in 1997 he became the chairman of the company. By 1998 Hughes owned 15 stations.

In 1999 Hughes's company, Radio One, went public. That means it became a publicly traded company on the stock market. By 2004 it had 70 stations. Hughes had become one of the most powerful African American women in the United States.

—Chapter 5—

Hit the Ground Running

The most successful entrepreneurs are often those who turn their interests into good ideas and profitable businesses.

Phil Knight was on the University of Oregon's track team when he was studying there in the 1950s. He was studying to be an accountant. The University of Oregon's track team and its coach, Bill Bowerman, were famous.

At that time there weren't very good track shoes made in the United States. Most runners used shoes made in Europe. A lot of them really liked the Adidas brand. Sometimes Bowerman worked with shoes at home to make them better. Then he would give them to his team members. He was always trying to improve sports equipment.

*Knight went to business school after graduating. In one class he was assigned to write a paper on a small business he found interesting. Knight wrote that it was possible to have a profitable business buying good-quality running shoes from Japan. The shoes would be cheaper than European shoes, and he could advertise them by asking a famous track star to wear them. Later, no one remembered the speech Knight said he gave to the class for the project.

  After business school, Knight traveled to Asia. In 1962 he went to Japan. While there, he visited a shoe factory. The managers gave him a tour. His hosts asked what company he worked for. He made up a name right there—Blue Ribbon Sports. It was a lucky meeting. The Japanese company wanted to export their Tiger brand shoes to the United States, and Knight wanted to distribute shoes in the* United States.

Knight returned to the United States to start his business selling Tiger brand shoes. But he had no money and no employees. Knight kept his day job as an accountant, and he hired a salesman, Jeff Johnson, to sell Tiger shoes. His goal was to beat the biggest name in the market: Adidas.

Johnson had an idea. He would give away free Tiger shirts to winners at track meets. Soon, Tiger shirts were everywhere. Not long after, Knight and Johnson opened the first store in the United States that sold Tiger shoes. Johnson handled most of the details of the business. Finally, in 1968, Knight quit his day job to become an employee at his own company.

In 1970 Knight discovered that the Japanese company that made Tiger shoes was trying to take over Blue Ribbon Sports. So he decided to start a new company. He needed money for investment, but no bank would give him a loan. So he borrowed money from friends and family instead.

One night Johnson woke up after dreaming of the company's new name: Nike. In Greek stories, Nike was the winged goddess of victory. A friend designed a new logo for the company— the "swoosh."

Bowerman had helped design shoes for Blue Ribbon Sports. In 1970 he had created one of his most famous designs, the waffle sole, by pouring a rubber mixture into his wife's waffle iron. The waffle sole helped change sports shoe design forever.

In 1967 Bowerman had written a small book called *Jogging*. That book helped make running a popular sport in the United States. Fueled by the growth of running as a sport, the Nike brand grew quickly through the 1970s. By 1980 Nike was the biggest athletic shoe company in the United States. In 1982 Nike signed basketball star Michael Jordan to wear Nike shoes. Air Jordans became the most popular athletic shoes in the United States.

Phil Knight, President and CEO of Nike

Nike was doing well, so Knight decided to take a long trip to China. But soon another sport came along: aerobics. Nike did not realize fast enough that aerobics was going to be a big business, so it did not design shoes for this new market. Nike's new competitor, Reebok, took a big chunk of its business. By 1985 Reebok had taken over as the most popular sports shoe in the United States. Knight returned to the United States and took charge of Nike again. He rebuilt the company by changing most of its top managers.

By 2005 Nike was back on top of the market. Over 40 percent of sports shoes in the United States were Nike shoes. Knight made Nike one of the biggest sports brands in the world. But you don't have to be the biggest to be successful. Many entrepreneurs are successful by working in a *niche,* or one part of, the market.

In the 1980s, Missy Park played sports in high school and college. She played basketball, lacrosse, and tennis. But she could not find women's sports clothing that fit well. The only clothes she could find were shaped for men's bodies, but made smaller for women. They were also made of cheap nylon and were ugly.

After college, Park went to California. She worked for a big sporting goods company for a few years. While there, she learned about the sporting goods industry. Park thought other women must be as unhappy as she was with uncomfortable sports clothes. She had saved 15,000 dollars, so she decided to start her own company. She later said, "I thought, if they can do it, I can do it."[2] She was 26 years old.

[2] SAN FRANCISCO CHRONICLE by HARRIET CHANG. Copyright 2004 by SAN FRANCISCO CHRONICLE. Reproduced with permission of SAN FRANCISCO CHRONICLE in the format Textbook via Copyright Clearance Center.

Park named her business Title Nine Sports. She started it in her home in 1989. At first, her garage was the warehouse. She packed boxes of sweatpants and running shorts at the kitchen table. The first years were hard. When she sent out her first catalog, she received only four orders. Later she sent out 30,000 catalogs and received only 100 orders. To keep the business going she borrowed money from friends. Her company didn't make a profit until 1994.

In 1996 she opened her first store. Over time, she shifted from offering only hiking and biking clothing to offering casual clothing too. Finally, 15 years after she started, her business was huge. She now sends out about 26 million catalogs a year.

Chapter 6

Stores Without Walls

Where do you buy things? For a long time, the answer was simple. If you needed to buy something, you went to the store. But several important American entrepreneurs who lived a century apart decided to change the way people buy things.

Aaron Montgomery Ward lived around stores most of his life. His father bought a general store in Michigan when he was about eight years old. When Ward was 14 he quit school to help support his family. When he was about 16 he went to work in a general store for five dollars a month. He was ambitious. Three years later he was the manager and was making 100 dollars a month.

*Ward moved to Chicago in 1865 and took a job in a retail store. Then he started to work as a traveling salesman. He often traveled to small towns in the Midwest.

Ward saw that people who lived in small towns had few choices about what they could buy. Most of the time there was only one store in each town. Many people did not like the stores in their towns.

At that time, railroads were quickly connecting different areas of the country. Ward came up with a new idea. He discovered he could sell to customers in rural areas by sending items by mail on the railroad. Customers could also place orders by mail. Then he would not need *middlemen,* people who bought from suppliers and then sold to customers. He could buy large quantities of goods for less. By doing so, Ward could lower the price of the* goods.

Chicago was an important railroad center. Ward tried to raise money while he worked for a wholesale merchant there. He also began stocking up on merchandise. But then a disaster came. The Chicago Fire swept across the city in 1871. It destroyed all of Ward's merchandise. But he didn't give up.

The next year, Ward and several partners finally started their new company. Ward was helped by his new wife, Elizabeth, and money her family lent him. At first the company sold mostly to farmers. After a few years Ward bought out his partners. Then he quit his job at the wholesaler to work full-time on his new business.

Aaron Montgomery Ward

Ward's company was the first business to sell general goods directly to customers by mail. Ward published catalogs filled with items buyers could choose from. Orders were filled at the warehouse in Chicago. Then they were delivered by railroad. Farmers and others who lived in rural areas finally had the same choices people in big cities had.

In 1889 the company name became Montgomery Ward & Company. Ward and his brother-in-law soon earned 12,000 dollars a year. In 1893 Ward sold his share of the business to his brother-in-law. He wanted to work on other things. When Ward died in 1913, the mail-order company he had started had 6,000 employees. Its sales were 40 million dollars a year. He had changed the way people bought things.

Ward used the new railroad system to change the way goods were sold. More than 100 years later, new technology would again change shopping habits. And two entrepreneurial companies tried to master this new world where the old rules did not apply—Amazon and eBay.

Jeff Bezos studied computer science and electrical engineering in college. After graduating in 1986 he worked on software for Wall Street companies. By 1994 he saw how fast the Internet was growing. He decided to sell things over the Internet.

Bezos thought about what he could sell. He studied the items sold on the Internet. He carefully thought about all the choices. Finally, he decided to sell books. He saw that there are millions of books, so no bookstore can carry all of them. Then he had to choose a place for his business. He picked Seattle, Washington. It was close to a huge book warehouse, and there were many computer workers there.

Bezos then picked the name of his company. He chose the name Amazon because it began with the letter *a*. It was easy to remember, and it carried the idea of something huge, like the Amazon River.

Bezos and his wife drove from New York to Seattle. While his wife drove, Bezos wrote his business plan. He later found investors to back up his plan. Finally, in June 1995, Amazon.com took its first order.

Bezos worked at giving customers the biggest choice for the lowest price. Then he sent their products to them quickly. Amazon offered over two million titles. At first Bezos thought he would keep his costs low by buying books from book wholesalers and then selling them on the Web site. But he discovered he needed better control of the process to guarantee good customer service. After a few years he started to build warehouses.

Amazon's warehouses were different from the kind Ward had. Everything was computerized. Computers told workers which items to take off the shelves and in what order. Then it told them how to pack the orders.

To grow quickly, Bezos borrowed millions of dollars. In 1998 Amazon began to sell CDs. Four years after it started, the company had sales of 610 million dollars. Later Amazon began selling toys and housewares.

In 1999 Bezos was named *Time* magazine's "Person of the Year." At age 35, he was one of the youngest persons to be named by *Time*. Online retail had not even existed ten years earlier. Bezos was the "king" of the Internet economy.

The problem was that Amazon didn't turn a profit. Many investors thought the Internet would get bigger every year. They thought they would make money at some point. But in 2000, the Internet "bubble" burst. Many Internet companies went out of business. Investors lost millions of dollars. People began to openly criticize Bezos and his plan. They said the company would never make money.

But Bezos and Amazon kept going. Bezos's idea was to become the most reliable and biggest Internet retailer as quickly as possible. Once it was the most popular, he thought, it would also become the most profitable. But for years the company lost a lot of money.

By 2001 Amazon had over six million customers. It had sold over six billion dollars worth of goods. But it was not until 2003 that Amazon was profitable. It finally earned more money than it spent.

On the way to becoming profitable, Bezos remade the way books were sold by using new technology.

To fight off the competition, Bezos had to keep investing in new technology. But Amazon had many competitors, like Internet giants Yahoo!, Google, and eBay.

Pierre Omidyar was born in Paris. His parents, who were from Iran, had moved to France to go to college. Omidyar and his family moved to the United States when he was six years old.

Omidyar always loved to work on computers. After studying computer science in college, he took a job as a computer programmer at one of Silicon Valley's first Internet companies.

Omidyar's girlfriend, Peg, collected Pez candy dispensers. She told him she was having a hard time finding a place to buy and sell the collectibles. So in 1995, eBay was born.

Omidyar wanted to make it more than just an online auction house. He wanted eBay to be a place of "community." He wanted people to use the Internet to come together.

Omidyar wanted to make a profit by keeping costs low. There were no warehouses or stores, and he offered a service people paid for over and over again. Sellers paid a small fee to list an item. Then buyers could bid on it. Two years after it started, eBay was one of the most popular shopping sites on the Internet.

The popularity of eBay spread like wildfire. The company had grown very fast—almost too fast. Omidyar was a computer programmer. He knew he did not have the experience to make the company grow. So he sold part of the company to an investment firm. The firm then hired Meg Whitman, a professional manager, to help move the company forward.

Whitman had worked as a product manager at many companies, such as Hasbro, Walt Disney, and Proctor & Gamble. When she went to work at eBay, her friends were surprised. Why would she go to work for a small Internet auction company? There had never been such a thing.

Whitman had to find a way to turn the small company into a powerhouse. There were no blueprints for such a project. It was unknown territory.

In some ways, eBay was a very simple business to run. It didn't have warehouses. It didn't have to buy anything. It didn't have to take orders, fill them, or deliver them. It was a Web site that brought buyers and sellers together.

A serious problem almost closed eBay forever. In 1999 the system crashed. The site was closed for 22 hours. Thousands of customer files were at risk. After that, Whitman knew she had to build a stronger site.

Under Whitman, eBay grew into one of the most profitable companies in the United States. In 1999 eBay had income of 5.7 million dollars. In 2004 it was 3.2 billion dollars. It was the fastest-growing business in history. Less than ten years after eBay started, it had more than 7,000 employees. In 2004 Whitman was named *Fortune* magazine's "Most Powerful Woman in American Business."

Not so long ago, people would pack up camels and mules. They would walk dusty trails for months to bring goods to the West. Ships would load up with cargo. They would sail for months to take merchandise to buyers. Now, buyers can go to a Web site almost anywhere and order goods directly from there. Who can imagine how trade will change in the future? Can you?